YOUR PASSPORT TO
KENYA

Kaitlyn Duling

Raintree is an imprint of Capstone Global Library Limited, a company incorporated in England and Wales having its registered office at 264 Banbury Road, Oxford, OX2 7DY – Registered company number: 6695582

www.raintree.co.uk
myorders@raintree.co.uk

Edited by Jamie Hudalla
Designed by Colleen McLaren
Original illustrations © Capstone Global Library Limited 2021
Originated by Capstone Global Library Ltd
Printed and bound in India

978 1 3982 0555 0 (hardback)
978 1 3982 0556 7 (paperback)

British Library Cataloguing in Publication Data
A full catalogue record for this book is available from the British Library.

Acknowledgements
We would like to thank the following for permission to reproduce photographs: AP Images: Kike Calvo, 9; iStockphoto: FernandoQuevedo, 23; Red Line Editorial: 5; Shutterstock Images: Byelikova Oksana, 20, Dmitry Burlakov, 17, Jen Watson, 19, Jlwarehouse, 27, Julinzy, cover (flag), Martin Mwaura, 13, mbrand85, 15, Natashadub, cover (map), photocosmos1, 28, Piu_ Piu, 6, Volodymyr Burdiak, cover (bottom), 16
Design Elements: iStockphoto, Shutterstock Images

We would like to thank Kefa M. Otiso, PhD, Professor of Geography at the Bowling Green State University in Ohio, USA, for his assistance in the preparation of this book.

Every effort has been made to contact copyright holders of material reproduced in this book. Any omissions will be rectified in subsequent printings if notice is given to the publisher.

All the internet addresses (URLs) given in this book were valid at the time of going to press. However, due to the dynamic nature of the internet, some addresses may have changed, or sites may have changed or ceased to exist since publication. While the author and publisher regret any inconvenience this may cause readers, no responsibility for any such changes can be accepted by either the author or the publisher.

CONTENTS

CHAPTER ONE
WELCOME TO KENYA!.................................... 4

CHAPTER TWO
HISTORY OF KENYA 8

CHAPTER THREE
EXPLORE KENYA.................................... 12

CHAPTER FOUR
DAILY LIFE 18

CHAPTER FIVE
HOLIDAYS AND CELEBRATIONS 22

CHAPTER SIX
SPORT AND RECREATION 26

GLOSSARY 30
FIND OUT MORE .... 3 I
INDEX 32

Words in **bold** are in the glossary.

WELCOME TO KENYA!

The narrow streets of Nairobi are crowded. Buses honk. Bikes zoom past. The air is full of food smells, such as cooked meat and fried doughnuts. At the edge of Kenya's capital city, elephants wander in a huge national park. Lions sleep in the shade. Past the park, there are villages. Children walk to school. Adults farm the fields.

Kenya is in East Africa. It shares borders with Ethiopia, Somalia, South Sudan, Tanzania and Uganda. Its eastern edge touches the Indian Ocean. From wide **savannahs** to tall mountain peaks, the country has many beautiful sites. In recent years, the population has grown quickly. There are now more than 50 million people living there. Many people are moving from the countryside to the cities.

MAP OF KENYA

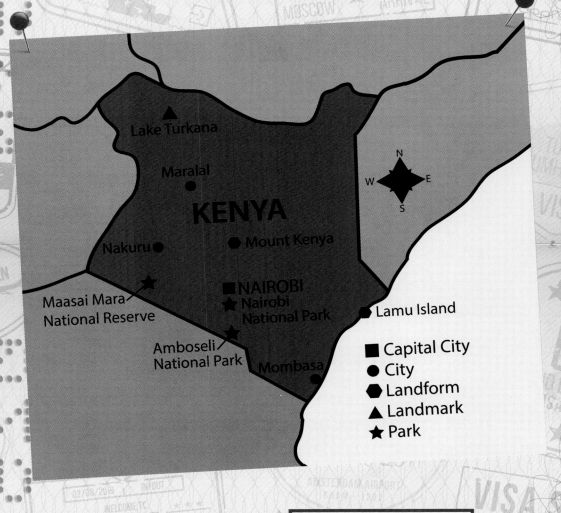

Lake Turkana

Maralal

KENYA

Nakuru

Mount Kenya

N
W E
S

Maasai Mara
National Reserve

■ NAIROBI
★ Nairobi
National Park

Lamu Island

Amboseli
National Park

Mombasa

■ Capital City
● City
⬡ Landform
▲ Landmark
★ Park

Explore Kenya's
cities and landmarks.

The Maasai often wear red clothes called *shukas*.

ONE NATION, MANY PEOPLE

Kenya's population includes many **ethnic groups**. Some, such as the Maasai and Turkana, live in small villages. The Maasai live in southern Kenya. They raise **livestock** for food and for sale. Many are strong warriors. Maasai wear red cotton clothes called *shukas*, which is a Swahili word. Swahili is one of Kenya's main languages.

FACT FILE

OFFICIAL NAME: .... REPUBLIC OF KENYA
POPULATION: 53,527,936
LAND AREA: .... 569,140 SQ. KM (219,746 SQ. MI)
CAPITAL: .... NAIROBI
MONEY: .... KENYAN SHILLING (KES)
GOVERNMENT: .... PRESIDENTIAL REPUBLIC
LANGUAGE: .... SWAHILI, OR KISWAHILI, AND ENGLISH
GEOGRAPHY: Kenya is located in Eastern Africa and borders the Indian Ocean. The country shares land borders with Ethiopia, Somalia, South Sudan, Tanzania and Uganda.
NATURAL RESOURCES: Kenya has gemstones such as sapphires and rubies. It also has limestone, salt and oil.

The Turkana live in north-west Kenya. They raise camels and cattle. People from Europe, South Asia and other parts of Africa live in the urban city areas of Kenya.

Music and storytelling are important in Kenya. Ethnic groups have long used songs, poems and stories to pass down their knowledge, beliefs and **customs**.

CHAPTER TWO

HISTORY OF KENYA

People have lived in the land that is now Kenya for millions of years. Fossils of early human bones and tools have been found in Kenya. People started moving to the area around the year 2000 **BCE**. They came from other parts of Africa.

The first Kenyans hunted for and gathered food. They moved around to find it. Some later began to keep livestock, such as sheep, goats and camels. In the 400s **CE**, Arab settlers moved into the coastal areas. They traded with Persia and India for ivory, rhino horns, gold and shells. These things were very valuable. Many people went to Kenya to trade for these items.

FIGHTING FOR CONTROL

The Arab settlers took control of the Kenyan coast and its people. They also influenced Kenyan culture. Swahili borrows many words from Arabic.

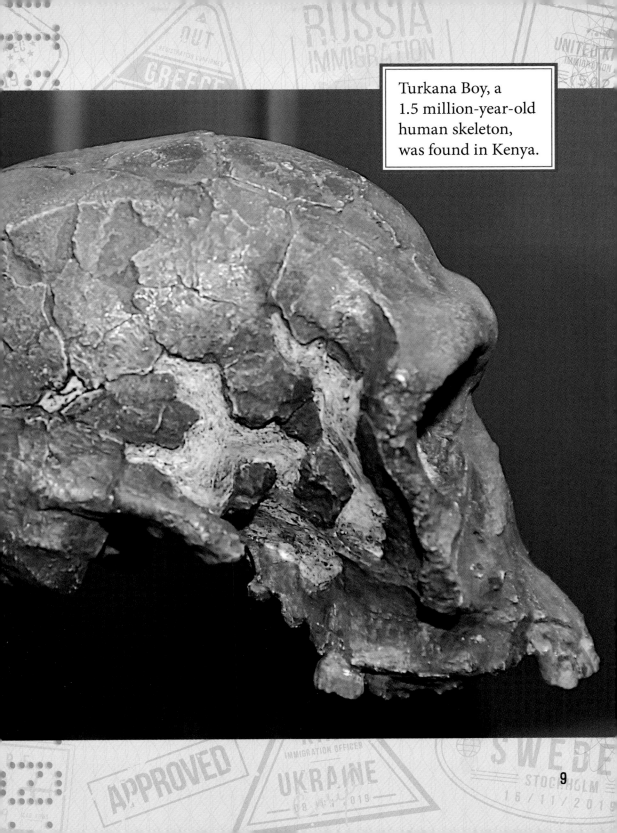

Turkana Boy, a
1.5 million-year-old
human skeleton,
was found in Kenya.

TIMELINE OF KENYAN HISTORY

400: Arabs settle in the coastal areas and develop trade stations.

1498: Portuguese explorers arrive in Kenya.

1505: The Portuguese and Arabs from the Middle East go to war over control of the region of Kenya.

1580s: The Portuguese defeat the Turks in a fight to control the region. The Portuguese continue to fight the Arabs. After 100 years, the Arabs win.

1895: Kenya becomes a British colony. Shortly after, British settlers move into the highlands.

1952: A group known as the Mau Mau begins fighting British settlers to protect their land.

1963: Kenya gains **independence** from Britain.

1978: Daniel arap Moi becomes president. He holds office for 24 years until 2002.

2010: A new set of laws is approved. It limits the powers of the president. The president can serve up to 2 terms of 5 years each.

In 1498, Portuguese explorers arrived on the Kenyan coast. They wanted to use trade routes on the Indian Ocean. The Portuguese gained power over the Kenyan coast. About 100 years later, the Islamic leader of Oman tried to do the same. For nearly 400 years, the Portuguese, Arabs and Turks all fought for control of Kenya.

INDEPENDENCE

In 1895, the British **colonized** Kenya. British and Indian settlers moved in. Britain also ruled India.

The British did not let most Kenyans participate in politics. The Kenyans had no power over their own region. In 1952, they rebelled against the British. They fought to gain control over their government. Kenya finally gained independence in 1963.

Kenya's government is now a presidential **republic**. Daniel arap Moi was president from 1978 to 2002. In 2010, Kenya passed a set of laws. Those laws limited the power of the president. The country now elects a president every five years.

FACT

In 2018, Kenya was the fourth-largest producer of flowers. Roses, lilies and other flowers are grown in Kenya. They are sold around the world.

CHAPTER THREE

EXPLORE KENYA

There is beauty everywhere in Kenya. Visitors can explore tall mountains and deep valleys. There are flat savannahs and sandy beaches. Coffee and tea farms stretch out across the countryside.

NATURAL SITES

Tourism is very important in Kenya. It brings in a lot of money. People travel from all over the world to visit the country. They go on wildlife **safaris** in Kenya's nature parks. The parks are full of large wild animals. Visitors can see lions, elephants and more.

Mount Kenya is the second-highest mountain in Africa. It is a popular site. The mountain is a volcano. It no longer erupts. The Kikuyu people live at the base of the mountain. They believe that it is the home of Ngai, their god.

People can climb
Mount Kenya.

CITIES TO VISIT

Kenya has large cities. Nairobi is the largest. Its name means "cold water" in the local Maasai language. There are houses and skyscrapers. More than 4 million people live there. Animals live there too. Nairobi National Park is inside the city limits. It is just 6.4 kilometres (4 miles) from the city centre. A fence separates the lions, rhinos and other animals from the city. Tourists also love to visit the city's museums. The Nairobi National Museum highlights Kenya's nature, history and art.

MOMBASA

Mombasa is the country's oldest and second-largest city. It was founded in 900 CE. More than 1 million people lived there as of 2016. It is on the edge of the Indian Ocean. Mombasa has the largest **port** in East Africa. It has long been a big trading centre. Today, tourists from across the globe travel to the city. They enjoy its beautiful beaches and plush hotels. Visitors can get to the city from Nairobi by train. They can see animals when the train passes through Tsavo National Park and Nairobi National Park.

Nairobi National Park is home to many wild animals.

Nakuru is another big city. People from Africa, Europe and Asia live there. The city is famous for its flamingos. Thousands of these pink birds live at Lake Nakuru.

Mount Kilimanjaro is the tallest mountain in Africa.

PARKS AND RESERVES

Kenya is full of wildlife outside its cities. In 1946, the country made its first national park. Today, there are 55 national parks and game reserves. Visitors can go on safaris to see large animals in the wild. The most famous park is the Maasai Mara National Reserve. There, people can see lions, leopards, buffalos, rhinos and elephants.

While in national parks, visitors must stop for animals crossing the road.

Visitors to Amboseli National Park get another amazing view. From the park, they can see Mount Kilimanjaro. It is the largest mountain in Africa. This mountain sits on the border of Kenya and Tanzania.

CHAPTER FOUR

DAILY LIFE

Most Kenyans are farmers. They grow crops such as corn. Farmers also keep cows and goats. They use most of the food to feed their families. Some farmers sell their food. Most people in rural areas cook their food using firewood. Water for cooking and bathing usually comes from nearby wells and rivers. Some groups, such as the Maasai, eat meat and drink milk from their cattle.

VILLAGES AND CITIES

The El Molo tribe is one of the smallest in Kenya. They live in a village on the shore of Lake Turkana. Their homes are huts made of reeds. They use spears and nets to catch fish in the lake. The El Molo also hunt hippos and crocodiles. Women weave baskets and make jewellery. There are villages like this one all across Kenya. Each village has unique music, dances, clothing and food. Some have their own languages too.

Some Kenyans grow and sell tea leaves.

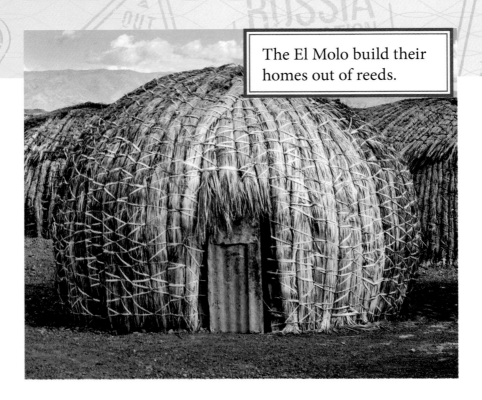

The El Molo build their homes out of reeds.

Most people live in rural areas, but cities are now growing. In Nairobi, many people work in offices. They drive to work or catch a bus or train. Some children ride bikes catch a bus to school. At weekends, many families gather together. They eat meals and go to church.

COMMON MEALS

Breakfast is usually a cup of tea or corn porridge with bread or potatoes. One popular Kenyan food is *chapati*. This is a flat wheat bread. *Ugali* is also common. It is stiff mash made of corn flour.

Ugali is usually eaten with spiced vegetables or meat stews. Stew vegetables often include spinach. Meat from cattle and goats is also popular. British, Arab and Indian foods have influenced Kenyan cooking. So Kenyans eat rice, chillies and curries. Kenyans also love juicy fruits, such as mangoes and coconuts. Special occasions are a time for *nyama choma*. That is Swahili for "roast meat".

UGALI

Ugali is a stiff corn mash often served with meat or vegetables. Kenyans usually eat *ugali* with their hands. They use it to scoop up and eat a small portion of a vegetable or meat stew. With the help of an adult, you can make this recipe at home.

Ingredients:
- 1 litre water
- 1 teaspoon of salt
- 250 g of white cornflour or millet

Method:
1. Pour water and salt into a saucepan.
2. Bring the water to a boil. Slowly stir in the cornflour.
3. Turn the heat to medium-low. Continue stirring, mashing lumps with a spoon. Do this for about 10 minutes.
4. The mush should be thick and pull away from the sides of the pan.
5. Remove from heat and allow to cool. After it cools, you can form the *ugali* into a ball and serve.

CHAPTER FIVE

HOLIDAYS AND CELEBRATIONS

There is no official religion in Kenya. However, most Kenyans are Christian. Islam is also widely practised in Kenya. About 83 per cent of Kenyans are Christian, and 11 per cent are Muslim. About 2 per cent practise African traditional religions, and another 2 per cent are not religious. Both Christian and Muslim holy days are national holidays. They include Christmas and Eid al-Fitr. Kenyan schools and some businesses are closed for these holidays.

THE INTERNATIONAL CAMEL DERBY

Every year, people come from far and wide to watch the camel derby. The race begins just outside the town of Maralal. There are different distances for each camel race. The region's finest camels gather at the starting line. The animals run through the desert. Riders try to balance on top of the one-humped camels. Camels are not harmed during the race. Whoever finishes the race first is the winner!

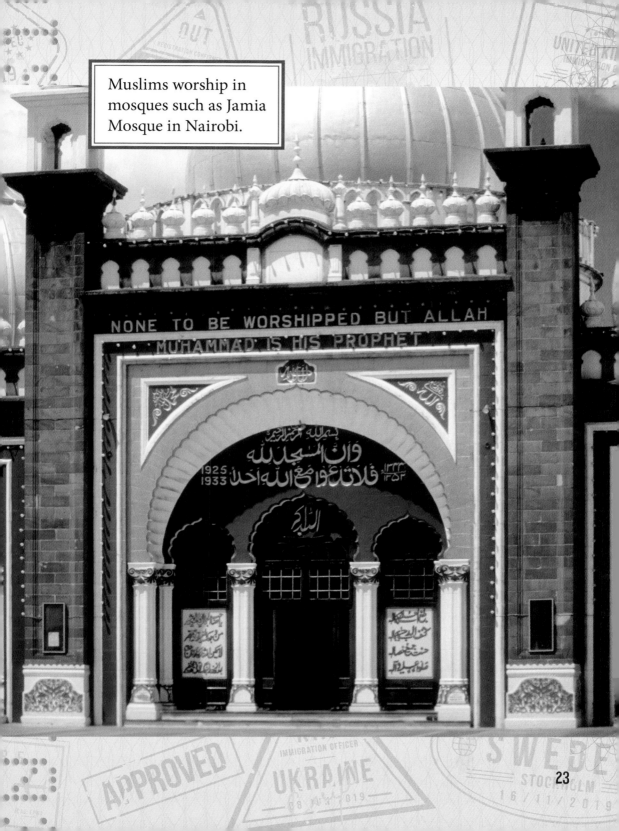

Muslims worship in mosques such as Jamia Mosque in Nairobi.

CELEBRATING INDEPENDENCE

Many national holidays in Kenya celebrate independence. Madaraka Day celebrates the 1963 election of Kenya's first African prime minister, who is the head of government. Mashujaa Day is also called Heroes' Day. It remembers people who fought for freedom. Jamhuri Day marks the day Kenya became fully independent. It is one of the most important days on the Kenyan calendar. People celebrate with feasts, parades, speeches and dancing.

FESTIVALS AND CARNIVALS

Each year, Kenyans celebrate traditions with festivals and carnivals. Some of these events are many days long. They feature delicious foods and fun music. Each November, the Lamu community hosts a week-long carnival on Lamu Island. There are donkey races and competitions. People read Swahili poetry. Participants paint their hands and arms with henna, a special dye. The detailed works of art wear off after a few weeks.

PUBLIC HOLIDAYS IN KENYA

NEW YEAR'S DAY: 1 January
GOOD FRIDAY*
EASTER MONDAY*
LABOUR DAY: 1 May
EID AL-FITR*
MADARAKA DAY: 1 June

MASHUJAA DAY: 20 October
JAMHURI (INDEPENDENCE) DAY: 12 December
CHRISTMAS DAY: 25 December
BOXING DAY: 26 December
*Dates vary

Mombasa Carnival is the biggest festival. At this event, people celebrate cultural **diversity** through floats, costumes, dances and music. People travel from all over Kenya to attend. Another large celebration is the three-day Maulidi festival. It is hosted by Muslim religious leaders and the National Museum of Kenya. Singing and dancing mark the birth of the Prophet Muhammad. Visitors and believers celebrate together.

FACT

Mombasa Carnival often ends with a boat race on the Indian Ocean.

SPORT AND RECREATION

Many Kenyans love to watch and play football. Kenyans also play rugby, cricket and wrestling. Board games, such as mancala, are also popular. Mancala is a traditional East African board game. It is played with small stones on a long wooden board. In Kenya, the game is called *Bao*.

WINNING MEDALS

Kenyan athletes compete around the world. Since 1956, Kenya has sent athletes to nearly every Summer Olympics. Over the years, they have won more than 100 Olympic medals.

Kenyans often compete in track and field events. They have been successful in long-distance running events. Kenyan athletes have won a few medals in boxing too.

Whether in cities or villages, children in Kenya love to play football.

Eliud Kipchoge is one of the best long-distance runners in the world.

Some of the most successful long-distance runners are from Kenya. In 2019, Eliud Kipchoge became the world-record holder for the fastest time running a marathon. He ran a marathon in less than two hours!

KOLOLO-I

In rural parts of Kenya, children may not have many toys or access to technology. They play games that use little or no equipment. To play *Kololo-i*, you will need six or more people and an open space.

1. Form a circle and join hands.
2. Move in a circle quickly while swinging hands.
3. One person chants these words: *Kololo-i howuee kanga*, which is similar to "Let's move".
4. The group chants these words: *Kololo-i howuee kanga*.
5. If two people drop hands at any point, they must leave the circle.
6. Two at a time must leave until only two people remain. Those two are the winners.

GLOSSARY

BCE/CE
BCE means Before Common Era, or before year one. CE means Common Era, or after year one.

colonize
take control of a foreign country

custom
tradition specific to a place or group

diversity
wide range of different people or things

ethnic group
people who share a common culture, race, language or nationality

independence
freedom a country has to govern itself

livestock
farm animals

port
place where ships are loaded and unloaded

republic
type of government where people elect their political leaders and president

safari
journey in which someone can witness wild animals in their natural habitat

savannah
grassy plain with very few trees

FIND OUT MORE

BOOKS

Africa (Investigating Continents), Christine Juarez (Raintree, 2018)

Africa (Mathalon Maps), Joanne Randolph (Raintree, 2017)

My Life in Kenya (A Child's Day in…), Patience Coster (Arcturus, 2019)

WEBSITES

kids.nationalgeographic.com/explore/countries/kenya
Explore more about Kenya with National Geographic.

www.bbc.co.uk/bitesize/clips/zrsgkqt
This BBC Bitesize video shows you more about the Kenyan countryside and its landscape.

www.kids-world-travel-guide.com/facts-about-kenya.html
This website has lots of interesting facts about Kenya.

INDEX

Amboseli National Park 17

Arabs 8, 10, 21

British 10, 11, 21

El Molo 18

holidays and festivals 22, 24–25

Kipchoge, Eliud 29

Lake Turkana 18

Maasai 6, 14, 18

Maasai Mara National Reserve 16

Moi, Daniel arap 10, 11

Mombasa 14, 25

Mount Kenya 12

Mount Kilimanjaro 17

Nairobi 4, 14, 20

Nakuru 15

Portuguese 10

Swahili 6, 8, 21, 24

Turkana 6–7

ugali (recipe) 21

OTHER BOOKS IN THIS SERIES

YOUR PASSPORT TO CHINA

YOUR PASSPORT TO ECUADOR

YOUR PASSPORT TO EL SALVADOR

YOUR PASSPORT TO ETHIOPIA

YOUR PASSPORT TO FRANCE

YOUR PASSPORT TO IRAN

YOUR PASSPORT TO PERU

YOUR PASSPORT TO RUSSIA

YOUR PASSPORT TO SPAIN